Let Us Draw Near

by

Andrew Murray

Rickfords Hill Publishing Ltd.

Published by
RICKFORDS HILL PUBLISHING LTD.
24 High Street, Winslow, Buckingham, MK18 3HF, UK.
www.rhpbooks.co.uk

First Published 1891
This edition 2023

Scripture quotations are taken from the American Standard Version.

ISBN: 978-1-905044-53-5

Printed and bound in Great Britain
by CPI Group (UK) Ltd, Croydon CR0 4YY

Preface

The twelve chapters that form this little book are part of a larger work that has just been published.* They are issued separately in the hope that they may bring the tidings that the Father would indeed have us live our life in His Presence, and that Christ is able to bring and keep us there, to some whom the larger work may not reach.

The passage of which these chapters are the exposition (Chapter 10:9–25) constitutes the very centre of the Epistle. It contains a summary of what had been taught in its first or doctrinal part, and indicates at the same time the chief thoughts which are to be enforced in the second half. Within the compass of a very few verses it gathers up all that has been said of our Blessed High Priest and His work, all that can be said of what we need fully to enjoy the fruit of that work, and all that has yet to be said in the Epistle of the influence its teaching is to exercise upon us. It makes all centre round the one thought: 'Let us draw nigh.' Let us, in the power of Christ's redemption, enter in and dwell in the Father's presence.

In the larger book I have endeavoured to point out how the state of the Hebrews was just what we find in the churches of our days. There is a lack of steadfastness, of

---

The Holiest of All: The Presence of God, the Sphere of Christ's Ministry in Heaven, and our Life and Service on Earth. A Devotional Exposition of the Epistle to the Hebrews (130 chapters).

growth, and of power, which arises from our not knowing Jesus aright. I have therefore tried to show, as the Epistle led, that the true knowledge of the wonderful and blessed truths of the divinity and humanity of our Lord; of His being our Leader and Forerunner in the path of obedience and perfect surrender to God's will; above all, of His heavenly Priesthood in the power of an endless life, and His having procured us perfect liberty of access and abode in God's Presence through His blood, gives a strength to our faith and hope, which enables us in very deed to obtain the promise and live as God would have us do. But I am not without hope that even this smaller volume may urge some to seek and discover what the treasure is that the Epistle contains, and help them to enter into the personal possession of that complete salvation our great High Priest waits and is able to bestow.

That the teaching of God's Holy Spirit may be the portion of all my readers, is my earnest prayer.

ANDREW MURRAY
26th September, 1891

Contents

	Preface	iii
1.	The Entrance into the Holiest	1
2.	Boldness through the Blood of Jesus	6
3.	The New and Living Way	11
4.	A Great Priest over the House of God	16
5.	With a True Heart	21
6.	The Fulness of Faith	26
7.	Our Hearts Sprinkled	31
8.	Our Body Washed	36
9.	Let Us Draw Near	41
10.	The Confession of Our Hope	46
11.	Let Us Provoke unto Love	51
12.	The Assembling Together	56
	Conclusion	61

Hebrews 10:19–25

19 Having therefore, brethren, boldness to enter into the holy place by the blood of Jesus,
20 by the way which he dedicated for us, a new and living way, through the veil, that is to say, his flesh;
21 and having a great priest over the house of God;
22 let us draw near with a true heart in fulness of faith, having our hearts sprinkled from an evil conscience, and our body washed with pure water:
23 let us hold fast the confession of our hope that it waver not; for he is faithful that promised:
24 and let us consider one another to provoke unto love and good works;
25 not forsaking the assembling of ourselves together, as the custom of some is, but exhorting one another; and so much the more, as you see the day drawing nigh.

It may help us the better to master the rich contents of this central passage, containing a summary of the whole Epistle, if we here give the chief thoughts it contains.

I. The four great Blessings of the new life:

1. The Holiest opened up.
2. Boldness in the Blood.
3. A New and Living Way.
4. The Great High Priest.

II. The four chief Marks of the true believer.

1. A True Heart.
2. Fulness of Faith.
3. A Heart sprinkled from an Evil Conscience.
4. The Body washed with Clean Water.

III. The four great Duties to which the opened Sanctuary calls:

1. Let us draw nigh (in the fulness of faith).
2. Let us hold fast the profession of our hope.
3. Let us consider one another to provoke unto love.
4. Let us not forsake the assembling of ourselves together.

1

The Entrance into the Holiest

"Having therefore, brethren, boldness to enter
into the Holy Place; let us draw near."
(10:19, 22)

Enter into the Holiest. With these words the second half of the Epistle begins. Hitherto the teaching has been mainly doctrinal. The glory of Christ's person and priesthood; of the heavenly sanctuary which He, through His own blood, has opened and cleansed and taken possession of for us; of the way of obedience and self-sacrifice which led Him up to the throne; has been unfolded. Now comes the practical part, and our duty to appropriate the great salvation that has been provided is summed up in the one thought: *Having boldness to enter into the Holiest; let us draw near.* Access to God's presence and fellowship, the right and the power to make that our abiding dwelling-place, to live our life there, has been provided in Christ: let us draw near, here let us abide. God does in very deed mean that every child of His should always dwell in His presence.

Enter into the Holiest. It is a call to the Hebrews to come out of that life of unbelief and sloth, that leads to a departing from the living God, and to enter into the promised land, the rest of God, a life in His fellowship and favour. It is a call to all lukewarm, half-hearted Christians, no longer to remain in the outer court of the tabernacle, content with the hope that their sins are pardoned. Nor even to be satisfied with having entered the Holy Place, and there doing the service of the tabernacle, while the veil still hinders the full fellowship with the living God and His love. It calls to enter in through the rent veil, into the place into which the blood has been brought, and where the High Priest lives, there to live and walk and work, always in the presence of the Father. It is a call to all doubting, thirsting believers, who long for a better life than they have yet known, to cast aside their doubts, and to believe that this is what Christ has indeed done and brought within the reach of each one of us: He has opened the way into the Holiest! This is the salvation which He has accomplished, and which He lives to apply in each of us, so that we shall indeed dwell in the full light of God's countenance.

Enter into the Holiest. This is, in one short word, the fruit of Christ's work, the chief lesson of the Epistle, the one great need of our Christian life, the complete and perfect salvation God in Christ gives us to enjoy.

Enter into the Holiest. What Holiest? To the reader who has gone with us through the Epistle thus far, it is hardly needful to say: No other than that very same into which Christ, when He had rent the veil in His death, entered through His own blood, to appear before the face of God for us. It is the Holiest, in which God dwelt, in which the priests, and even the high priest, might not dwell, into which Jesus entered for us, in which we now are to dwell.

That Holiest of All is the heavenly place; but not heaven, as it is ordinarily understood, as a locality, distinct and separate from this earth. The heaven of God is not limited in space in the same way as a place on earth. There is a heaven above us, the place of God's special manifestation. But there is also a spiritual heaven, as omnipresent as God Himself. Where God is, is heaven; the heaven of His presence includes this earth too. The Holiest into which Christ entered, and into which He opened the way for us, is the inaccessible (to the natural man) light of God's holy presence and love, full union and communion with Him. Into that Holiest the soul can enter by the faith that makes us one with Christ. There it can abide continually, because Jesus, as we saw in Chapter 7, abideth continually. The Holy Spirit, who first signified that the way of the Holiest was not yet open; through whom Jesus shed the blood that opened the way; who, on the day of Pentecost, witnessed in the heart of the disciples, that it was now indeed open; waits to signify to us what it means to enter in, and to bring us in. He lifts the soul up into the Holiest; He brings the Holiest down into the soul. In the power of the Holy Spirit we can now dwell in the nearness and presence of God.

Enter into the Holiest. Oh, the glory of the message. For fifteen centuries Israel had a sanctuary with a Holiest of All, into which, under pain of death, no one might enter. Its one witness was: man cannot dwell in God's presence, cannot abide in His fellowship. And now, how changed is all! As then the warning sounded: *No admittance! Enter not!* so now the call goes forth: *Enter in!* the veil is rent; the Holiest is open; God waits to welcome you to His bosom. Henceforth, you are to live with Him. This is the message of the Epistle: 'Child! thy Father longs for thee to enter, to dwell, and to go out no more for ever.'

Oh, the blessedness of a life in the Holiest! Here the Father's face is seen and His love tasted. Here His holiness is revealed, and the soul made partaker of it. Here the sacrifice of love and worship and adoration, the incense of prayer and supplication, is offered in power. Here the soul, in God's Presence, grows into more complete oneness with Christ, and into more entire conformity to His likeness. Here, in union with Christ in His unceasing intercession, we are emboldened to take our place as intercessors, who can have power with God and prevail. Here the outpouring of the Spirit is known as an ever-streaming, overflowing river, from under the throne of God and the Lamb. Here the soul mounts up as on eagles' wings, the strength is renewed, and the blessing and the power and the love are imparted with which God's priests can go out to bless a dying world. Here each day we may experience the fresh anointing with which we go out to be the bearers and the witnesses and the channels of God's salvation to men, the living instruments through whom our Blessed King works out His will and final triumph.

O Jesus! our great High Priest, let this be our life!

1. "One thing have I desired of the LORD, that will I seek after; that I may dwell in the house of the LORD **all the days of my life**, to behold the beauty of the LORD, and to enquire in His temple." (Psalm 27:4) Here this prayer is fulfilled.

2. "Did not Jesus say, 'I am the door of the sheepfold'? What to us is the sheepfold, dear children? It is the heart

THE ENTRANCE INTO THE HOLIEST

of the Father, whereunto Christ is the gate that is called Beautiful. O children, how sweetly and how gladly has He opened that door into the Father's heart, into the treasure-chamber of God! And there within He unfolds to us the hidden riches, the nearness and the sweetness of companionship with Himself."—Tauler.

3. We have read of a man's father or friends purchasing and furnishing a house for a birthday or a wedding gift. They bring him there, and, handing the keys, say to him: "This is now your home." Child of God! the Father opens unto thee the Holiest of All, and says: "Let this now be thy home." What shall our answer be?

2

Boldness Through the Blood of Jesus

"Having therefore, brethren, boldness to enter
into the Holy Place; Let us draw near."
(10:19, 22)

Enter into the Holiest. This word brought us the message of the Epistle. Christ has in very deed opened the Holiest of All for us to enter in and to dwell there. The Father would have His children with Him in His holy home of love and fellowship, abiding continually all the time. The Epistle seeks to gather all in. Having boldness to enter, *let us draw near!*

It may be that some, as in the study of the Epistle the wondrous mystery of the way into the Holiest now opened was revealed to them, have entered in; they have said in faith, Lord my God, I come. Henceforth I would live in Thy secret place, in the Holiest of All. And yet they fear. They are not sure whether the great High Priest has indeed taken them in. They know not for certain whether they will be faithful, always abiding within the veil. They have not yet grasped what it means—*having boldness to enter in.*

And there may be others, who have with longing, wistful hearts heard the call to enter in, and yet have not the courage to do so. The thought that a sinful worm can every day and all the day dwell in the Holiest of All is altogether too high. The consciousness of feebleness and failure is so strong, the sense of personal unfaithfulness so keen, the experience of the power of the world and circumstances, of the weakness of the flesh and its efforts so fresh, that for them there is no hope of such a life. Others may rejoice in it, they must even be content without it. And yet the heart is not content.

To both such, those who have entered but still are full of fears, and those who in fear do not enter, the Holy Spirit speaks—*Today, if you shall hear His voice, harden not your hearts. Having boldness in the blood of Jesus to enter into the Holiest, let us draw nigh.* The boldness with which we are to enter is not, first of all, a conscious feeling of confidence; it is the objective God-given right and liberty of entrance of which the blood assures us. The measure of our boldness is the worth God attaches to the blood of Jesus. As our heart reposes its confidence on that in simple faith, the feeling of confidence and joy on our part will come too, and our entrance will be amid songs of praise and gladness.

Boldness in the blood of Jesus. Everything depends upon our apprehension of what that means. If the blood be to us what it is to God, the boldness which God means it to give will fill our hearts. As we saw in Chapter 9, what the blood has effected in rending the veil and cleansing the heavens, and giving Jesus, the Son of Man, access to God, will be the measure of what it will effect within us, making our heart God's sanctuary, and fitting us for perfect fellowship with the Holy One. The more we honour the blood in its infinite worth, the more will it prove its mighty energy and efficacy, opening heaven to us and in us, giving us, in divine power, the real living experience of what the entrance into the Holiest is.

The blood of Jesus. The life is the blood. As the value of this life, so the value of the blood. In Christ there was the life of God; infinite as God is the worth and the power of that blood. In Christ there was the life of man in its perfection; in His humility, and obedience to the Father, and self-sacrifice, that which made Him unspeakably well pleasing to the Father. That blood of Jesus, God and Man, poured out in a death that was a perfect fulfilment of God's will, and a perfect victory over all the temptations of sin and self, effected an everlasting atonement for sin, and put it for ever out of the way, destroying death and him that had the power of it. Therefore it was, that in the blood of the everlasting covenant Jesus was raised from the dead; that in His own blood, as our Head and Surety, He entered heaven; and that that blood is now for ever in heaven, in the same place of honour as *God the Judge of all, and Jesus the Mediator* (12:24). It is this blood, now in heaven before God for us, that is our boldness to enter in, even into the very Holiest of All.

Beloved Christian! The blood of Jesus! The blood of the Lamb! O think what it means. God gave it for your redemption. God accepted it when His Son entered heaven and presented it on your behalf. God has it for ever in His sight as the fruit, the infinitely well-pleasing proof, of His Son's obedience unto death. God points you to it, and asks you to believe in the divine satisfaction it gives to Him, in its omnipotent energy, in its everlasting sufficiency. Oh, will you not this day believe that that blood gives you, sinful and feeble as you are, liberty, confidence, boldness

BOLDNESS THROUGH THE BLOOD

to draw nigh, to enter the very Holiest? Yes, believe it, that the blood, and the blood alone, but the blood most surely, brings you into the very presence, into the living and abiding fellowship, of the everlasting God. And let your response to God's message concerning the blood, and the boldness it gives you, be nothing less than this, that this very moment you go with the utmost confidence, and take your place in the most intimate fellowship with God. And if your heart condemn you, or coldness or unbelief appear to make a real entrance impossible, rest not till you believe and prove to the full the power of the blood in very deed to bring you nigh. *Having boldness by the blood of Jesus, let us draw near!*

1. Which is now greater in your sight; your sin or the blood of Jesus? There can be but one answer. Then draw nigh, and enter in, into the Holiest of All. As your sin has hitherto kept you back, let the blood now bring you nigh. And the blood will give you the boldness and the power to abide.

2. "One drop of that blood, coming out of the Holiest on the soul, perfects the conscience, makes that there is no more conscience of sin, and enables us to live in the fellowship of God and His Son. Such a soul, sprinkled with the blood, is able to enjoy the heavenly treasures, and to accomplish the heavenly service of the living God."

3. And that blood, such is its heavenly cleansing power, can keep the soul clean. "If we walk in the light, as He is in the light," if we live in the Holiest, in the light of His countenance, "we have fellowship one with another, and

the blood of Jesus Christ, His Son, cleanseth us from all sin," so that no sin touch us, whereby we lose the fellowship with the Father.

4. Understand how the Father's heart longs that His children draw near to Him boldly. He gave the blood of His Son to secure it. Let us honour God, and honour the blood, by entering the Holiest with great boldness.

5. So near, so very near to God,
   More near I cannot be,
  For in the person of His Son
   I am as near as He.

3

The New and Living Way

"Having therefore, brethren, boldness to enter into the Holy Place by the blood of Jesus, by the way which He dedicated for us, a new and living way, through the veil, that is to say, His flesh;
Let us draw near." (10:19, 22)

The Holiest of All is opened for us to enter in and appear before God, to dwell and to serve in His very presence. The blood of the one Sacrifice for ever, taken into heaven to cleanse away all sin for ever, is our title and our boldness to enter in. Now comes the question, What is the way that leads up and through the opened gate, and in which we have to walk if we are to enter in? This way, the only way, the one infallible way, is a *new and living way, which Jesus dedicated for us, through the veil, that is to say, His flesh.* The boldness we have through the blood is the right or liberty of access Jesus won for us, when we regard His death as that of our Substitute, who did what we can never do—made redemption of transgressions, and put away sin for ever. *The new and living way, through the rent veil, that is, His flesh*, has reference to His death, regarded as that of our Leader and Forerunner, who opened up a path to God, in which He first walked Himself, and then draws us to follow Him. The death of Jesus was not only the dedication or inauguration of the new sanctuary and of the new covenant, but also of the new way into the holy presence and fellowship of God. Whoever in faith accepts of the blood He shed as His boldness of entrance, must accept, too, of the way He opened up as that in which he walks.

And what was that way? *The way through the veil, that is, His flesh.* The veil is the flesh. The veil that separated man from God was the flesh, human nature under the power of sin. Christ came in the likeness of sinful flesh, and dwelt with us here outside the veil. *The Word was made flesh. He also Himself in like manner partook of flesh and blood.* In the days of His flesh, He was tempted like as we are; He offered prayer and supplication with strong crying and tears. He learned obedience even to the death. Our will is our life. He gave up His own will to the death to seek God's will alone. Through the rent veil of His flesh, His will, His life, as yielded up to God in death, He entered into the Holiest. *Being made in likeness of men, He humbled Himself, becoming obedient even unto death. Wherefore also God highly exalted Him.* Through the rent veil He rose to the throne of God. And this is the way He dedicated for us. In the death to our own will we live to God and His will. The very path in which, as our Substitute, He accomplished redemption, is the path which He opened for us to walk in, the path of obedience to the will of God. "Christ suffered for you, leaving you an example that ye should follow His steps." Christ our High Priest is as literally and fully Leader and Forerunner as He is Substitute and Redeemer.

THE NEW AND LIVING WAY

His way is our way. As little as He could open and enter the Holiest for us, except in His path of suffering and obedience and self-sacrifice, as little can we enter in unless we walk in the same path. Jesus said as much of His disciples as of Himself: *Except a corn of wheat fall into the ground, and die, it abideth alone. He that hateth his life in this world shall keep it unto life eternal.* Paul's law of life is the law of life for every believer: *Bearing about in the body the dying of Jesus, that the life also of Jesus may be manifested in our body.* The way into the Holiest is the way of the rent veil, the way of sacrifice and of death. There is no way for our putting away sin from us but the way of Jesus; whoever accepts His finished work accepts what constitutes its spirit and its power; it is for every man as for the Master—to put away sin by the sacrifice of self. Christ's death was something entirely new, and so too His resurrection life, a life out of death such as never had been known. This new death and new life constitute the new and living way, in which we are to walk—a new way of living in which we draw nigh to God.

Even as when Christ spoke of taking His flesh as daily food, so here, where the Holy Spirit speaks of taking the rent veil of His flesh as our daily life, many say: *This is a hard saying; who can hear it? Who then can be saved?* To those who are willing and obedient and believe, all things are possible, because it is *a new and living way. A new way.* The word means ever fresh, a way that never decays or waxes old (8:13), but always retains its first perfection and freshness. It is the way which Jesus opened up, when He took away the first, that He might establish the second (10:9), and showed how not burnt sacrifices, but the sacrifice of our own will, to do God's will, is what delights God.

A living way. A way always needs a living man to move upon it; it does not impart either life or strength. This way, the way of obedience and suffering and self-sacrifice and death, however hard it appears, and to nature utterly impossible, is a living way. It not only opens a track, but supplies the strength to carry the traveller along. It acts in the power of the endless life, in which Christ was made a High Priest. We saw how the Holy Spirit watches over the way into the Holiest, and how He, as the eternal Spirit, enabled Christ, in opening the way, to offer Himself without spot unto God; it is He whose mighty energy pervades this way, and inspires it with life divine. As we are made partakers of Christ, as we come to God through Him, His life, the law of the Spirit of life in Christ Jesus, takes possession of us, and in His strength we follow in the footsteps of Christ Jesus. The way into the Holiest is the living way of perfect conformity to Jesus, wrought in us by His Spirit.

The new and living way through the rent veil into the Holiest. We now know what it is: it is the way of death. Yes, the way of death is the way of life. The only way to be set free from our fallen nature, with the curse and power of sin resting on it, is to die to it. Jesus denied Himself, would do nothing to please that nature He had taken, sinless though it was in Him. He denied it; He died to it. He gave up His own will to seek nothing but the will of God. This was to Him the path of life. And this is to us the living way. Accept God's will in every providence. Obey God's will in every command of nature as His word. Seek God's perfect will in every leading of His Spirit. Say, I am come to do Thy will, O God. And let God's will be the one aim of thy life. It will be to us as it was to Him, though it lead through death—the path to God and to life.

THE NEW AND LIVING WAY

As we know Him in the power of His resurrection, He leads us into the conformity to His death. He does it in the power of the Holy Spirit. So His death and His life, the new death and the new life of deliverance from sin, and fellowship with God, which He inaugurated, His death to His own will, and His abiding in God's will, work in us, and we are borne along on the will of God, as He was, to where He is. *Having therefore boldness to enter in by the new and living way, let us draw nigh.*

1. When first a believer avails himself of the boldness he has in the blood, and enters into the Holiest, he does not understand all that is meant by the new and living way. It is enough if his heart is right, and he is ready to deny himself and take up his cross. In due time it will be revealed what the full fellowship is with His Lord in the way He opened up, of obedience unto death.

2. The new and living way is not only the way for once entering in, but the way for a daily walk, entering ever deeper into God's love and will.

3. The way of life is the way of death. This fallen life, this self, is so sinful and so strong, there is no way of deliverance but by death. But, praise God! the way of death is the way of life; in the power of Christ's resurrection and indwelling we dare to walk in it.

4. Let each who longs to dwell in the secret of God's presence all the day, now, at once, and once for all, accept and enter on the new and living way: Jesus, by the Holy Spirit, will keep and lead you in it.

4

A Great Priest over the House of God

"And having a great Priest over the house of God;
let us draw near." (10:21, 22)

We said before that in the symbols of the Mosaic worship there were specially four things that, as types of the mystery of the coming redemption, demand attention. These are—the Sanctuary, the Blood, the Way into the Holiest, the Priest. The first three, all heavenly things, we have had; we now come to the fourth, the chief and the best of all—a living Person, Jesus, a great High Priest over the House of God. The knowledge of what He has won for me, the entrance into the Holiest; of the work He did to win it, the shedding of His blood; of the way in which I am to enter into the enjoyment of it all—all this is very precious. But there is something better still: it is this, that the living, loving Son of God is there personally to receive me, and make me partaker of all the blessedness that God has for me. This is the chief point: we have such a High Priest, who sat down on the right hand of the majesty in the heavens. Wherefore, brethren, having a great Priest over the house of God, let us draw near.

And what is now the work we need Jesus to do for us?

Has it not all been done? The Holiest is opened. Boldness through the blood has been secured. The living way has been dedicated to carry us in. What more is there that Jesus has to do for us? Nothing more; it has all been finished, once and for ever. And why is it then we are pointed to Him as the great Priest over the house of God? It is because, above all, we need Himself, the living Jesus, to make that work all life and truth in us, yea, Himself to be its life and truth in us. And what is it we may expect of Him? What we need, and what we must look to Him for is this, so to work in us that the work He has done for us may be made real within us, as a personal experience of the power of an endless life in which He was constituted Priest. Because He liveth ever, we read, He is able to save completely. Salvation is a subjective, experimental thing—manifest in the peace and holiness of heart He gives. We, our life, our inner man, our heart, our will and affections, are to be delivered from the power of sin, and to taste and enjoy the putting away of sin as blessed experience. In our very heart we are to find and feel the power of His redemption. As deep and strong as sin proved itself, in its actual power and its mastery within us, is Jesus to prove the triumph of redeeming grace.

His one work as Priest over the house of God is to bring us into it, and enable us to live there. He does this by bringing God and the soul into actual harmony, sympathy, and fellowship with each other. We saw in Chapter 8, how, as Minister of the sanctuary, He does all that is to be done in heaven with God; how, as Mediator of the new covenant, He does all that is to be done here on earth, in our heart; the one as effectually as the other. The two offices are united in the one great Priest; in each act of His He unites both functions, to the soul that knows what to expect, and trusts Him, for it. Every movement of Jesus on our behalf in the presence of God can have its corresponding movement in the heart of man.

And how is this effected?—In virtue of His union with us, and our union with Him. Jesus is the Last Adam; the new Head of the race. He is it in virtue of His real humanity, having in it the power of true divinity that filleth all. Just as Adam was our forerunner into death, and we have all the power of his sin and death working in us and drawing us on, so we have Jesus as our Forerunner into God's presence, with all the power of His death and His resurrection-life working in us, and drawing and lifting us with divine energy into the Father's presence. God has no delight in a fellowship with anything but the image of His Beloved Son. There can be no true worship or drawing nigh to God except as we are likeminded to Christ, and come with His spirit and disposition in us. And this is now His work, as High Priest bringing us nigh to God, that He breathes His own disposition in us, and we draw near to God, in living union with Him. Yes, Jesus, with His divine, His heavenly life, in the power of the throne on which He is seated, has entered into the deepest ground of our being, where Adam, where sin, do their work, and is there, unceasingly carrying out His work of lifting us heavenward into God's presence, and of making God's heavenly presence here on earth our portion.

And why is it we enjoy this so little? And what is needed that we come to its full enjoyment? And how can Jesus truly be to us a great High Priest, giving us our actual life in the Holiest of All? One great reason of failure is what the Epistle so insists on: our ignorance of the spiritual perfection-truth it seeks to teach, and specially of what the Holy Spirit witnesseth of the way into the Holiest. And what we need is just this, that the Holy Spirit Himself, that Jesus in the Holy Spirit, be waited on, and accepted, and trusted to do the work in power. Do keep a firm hold of this truth, that when our great High Priest once for all entered the Holiest, and sat down on the throne, it was the Holy Ghost sent down in His power into the hearts of His disciples, through whom the heavenly High Priest became a present and an indwelling Saviour, bringing down with Him into their hearts the presence and the love of God. That pentecostal gift, in the power of the glorified Christ, is the one indispensable channel of the power of Jesus' priesthood. Nothing but the fulness of the Spirit in daily life, making Jesus present within us, abiding continually, can keep us in the presence of God as full experience. Jesus is no outward High Priest, who can save us as from a distance. No, as the Last Adam, He is to us nowhere, if He is not in us. The one reason why the truth of His Heavenly Priesthood is so often powerless, is because we look upon it as an external, distant thing, a work going on in heaven above us. The one cure for this evil is to know that our great Priest over the house of God is the glorified Jesus, who in the Holy Spirit is present in us, and makes His presence and power in heaven by the Holy Spirit to be as real within us here as it is above us there.

He is Priest over the house of God, the place where God dwells. We are His house too. And as surely as Jesus ministers in the sanctuary above, He moment by moment ministers in the sanctuary within. *Wherefore, brethren, having,*—not only in gift, not only in the possession of right and thought, but in our hearts, in our inmost being,—*having a great Priest over the house of God, let us draw near.* Let Jesus Himself on the throne, in His power and love, be the one desire, and hope, and joy of our hearts: He will maintain His work in us as wonderfully as He has accomplished it for us.

1. *Having a great Priest!* You know a great deal of Jesus, but do you know this, that His chief, His all-comprehensive work, is to bring you near, oh, so near, to God? Has He done this for you? If not, ask Him, trust Him for it.

2. It is Jesus Himself I want. He alone can satisfy me. It is in the holy faith of Jesus, the compassionate sympathiser, in the holy love of Jesus, who calls us brethren, that we can draw near to God. It is in a heart given up, with its trust and love and devotion, to Jesus, that the presence of God will be felt.

3. *We have such a High Priest!* Yes, say, I have Him; in all His power and love He is mine; and yield to Him to do His work. He abideth continually: therefore we can abide continually too in the blessed life, in the secret of God's presence.

5

With a True Heart

"Let us draw near with a true heart." (10:22)

We have been looking at the four great blessings of the new worship by which God encourages us to draw near to Him. We shall now see what the four chief things are that God seeks for in us as we come to Him. Of these the first is, *a true heart.*

In man's nature the heart is the central power. As the heart is, so is the man. The desire and the choice, the love and the hatred of the heart prove what a man is already, and decide what he is to become. Just as we judge of a man's physical character, his size and strength and age and habits, by his outward appearance, so the heart gives the real inward man his character; and "the hidden man of the heart" is what God looks to. God has in Christ given us access to the secret place of His dwelling, to the inner sanctuary of His presence and His heart; no wonder that the first thing He asks, as He calls us unto Him, is the heart—a true heart; our inmost being must in truth be yielded to Him, true to Him.

True religion is a thing of the heart, an inward life. It is only as the desire of the heart is fixed upon God, the whole heart seeking for God, giving its love and finding its joy in God, that a man can draw near to God. The heart of man was expressly planned and created and endowed with all its powers, that it might be capable of receiving and enjoying God and His love. A man can have no more of religion, or holiness, or love, or salvation, or of God, than he has in his heart. As much as a man has of the inward heart religion, so much has he of salvation, and no more. As far as Christ through His Spirit is within the heart, making the thoughts and will likeminded with Himself, so far can a man's worship and service be acceptable to God. The Kingdom of God consists entirely in the state of the heart. Therefore God can ask for nothing else and nothing less than the heart—than a true heart.

What the word true means we see from the use of it made previously (8:2 and 9:24), *the true tabernacle*, and, *the Holy Place*, which are figures of *the true*. The first tabernacle was only a figure and a shadow of the true. There was, indeed, a religious service, and worship, but it had no real abiding power; it could not make the worshipper perfect. *The very image*, the substance and reality, of the heavenly things themselves, were only brought by Christ. And God now asks that, to correspond with the true sanctuary, there shall be a true heart. The old covenant, with its tabernacle and its worship, which was but a shadow, could not put the heart of Israel right. In the new covenant God's first promise is, *I will write my law in the heart: a new heart will I give thee.* As He has given His Son, full of grace and truth, in the power of an endless life, to work all in us as the Mediator of a new covenant, to write His law in our hearts, He calls us to draw nigh with *a true heart.*

God asks for the heart. Alas, how many Christians serve Him still with the service of the old covenant! There are seasons for Bible-reading and praying and church-going. But when one notices how speedily and naturally and happily, as soon as it is freed from restraint, the heart turns to worldly things, one feels how little there is of the heart in it: it is not the worship of a true heart, of the whole heart. The heart, with its life and love and joy, has not yet found in God its highest good. Religion is much more a thing of the head and its activities, of imagination and conception and wishes, which are but the old figures and shadows over again, than of the heart and its life; much more a thing of the human will and its power, than of that Spirit which God gives within us. The Spirit of Jesus makes every word of confession of sin, or of surrender to God's will, every act of trust in His grace, a living reality, the true expression of our inmost being. This constitutes the true heart.

The invitation comes: *Let us draw near with a true heart.* Let no one hold back for fear, "my heart is not true." There is no way for obtaining the true heart, but by acting it. God has given you, as His child, a new heart—a wonderful gift, if you but knew it. Through ignorance or unbelief or disobedience it has grown feeble and withered; its beating can, nevertheless, still be felt. The Epistle, with its solemn warnings and its blessed teaching, has come to bring arousing and healing. Even as Christ said to the man with the withered hand, Stand forth, He calls to you from His throne in heaven, Rise, and come and enter in with a true heart. As you hesitate, and look within to feel and to find out if the heart is true, and in vain seek to do what is needed to make it true, He calls again, *Stretch forth thy hand.* When He spake that to him of the withered arm, whom He had called to rise up and stand before Him, the man felt the power of Jesus' eye and voice, and he stretched it forth. Do thou, likewise, stretch forth, lift up, reach out that withered heart of thine, that has so been cherishing its own impotence,—stretch forth, and it will be made whole. In the very act of obeying the call to enter in, it will prove itself a true heart—a heart ready to obey and to trust its blessed Lord, a heart ready to give up all, and find its life in the secret of His presence. Yes, Jesus, the great Priest over the house of God, the Mediator of the new covenant, with the new heart secured thee, calls, *Draw nigh with a true heart.*

During these last years God has been rousing His people to the pursuit of holiness, that is, to seek the entrance into the Holiest, a life in full fellowship with Himself, the Holy One. In the teaching which He has been using to this end, two words have been very much in the foreground— Consecration and Faith. These are just what are here put first—a true heart and the fulness of faith. The true heart is nothing but true consecration, the spirit that longs to live wholly for God, that gladly gives up everything that it may live wholly for Him, and that above all yields up itself, as the key of the inner life, into His keeping and rule. True religion is an inward life, in the power of the Holy Spirit. The true heart does indeed enter into the true sanctuary, the blessed secret of God's presence, to abide there all the life through. Let us enter in into the inner sanctuary of God's love, and the Spirit will enter into the inner sanctuary of our love, into our heart. Let us draw nigh with a true heart—longing, ready, utterly given up to desire—and receive the blessing.

1. If you look at your own constitution, you see how the head and the heart are the two great centres of life and action. Much thought and study make the head weary. Strong emotion or excitement affects the heart. It is the heart God asks—the power of desire and affection and will. The head and the heart are in partnership. God tells us that the heart must rule and lead, that it is the heart He wants. Our religion has been too much that of the head— hearing and reading and thinking. Let us beware of allowing these to lead us astray. Let them stand aside at times. Let us give the heart time to assert its supremacy. Let us draw nigh with a true heart.

2. *A true heart*—true in what it says that it thinks of itself; true in what it says that it believes of God; true in what it professes to take from God and to give to Him.

3. It is the heart God wants to dwell in. It is in the state of the heart God wants to prove His power to bless. It is in the heart the love and the joy of God are to be known. Let us draw near with a true heart.

6

The Fulness of Faith

"Let us draw near... in fulness of faith." (10:22)

This translation, *the fulness of faith*, is not only more correct than that of "full assurance of faith," but much more significant. Full assurance of faith refers only to the strength and confidence with which we believe. The truth we accept may be very limited and defective, and our assurance of it may be more an undoubting conviction of the mind than the living apprehension of the heart. In both respects the fulness of faith expresses what we need,—a faith that includes objectively all that God offers it in its fulness, and subjectively all the powers of our heart and life in their fulness. *Let us draw near, in fulness of faith.*

Here, if anywhere, there is indeed need of fulness of faith, that we may take in all the fulness of the provision God has made, and of the promises that are waiting for us to inherit. The message comes to a sinful man that he may have his continual abode in the *Most Holy*; that, more real and near than with his nearest earthly friend, he may live in unbroken fellowship with the Most High God. He is assured that the *blood of Christ* can cleanse his conscience in such power that he can draw nigh to God with a perfect conscience and with undoubting confidence, and can ask and expect to live always in the unclouded light of God's face. He receives the assurance that the power of the Holy Ghost, coming from out of the Holiest, can enable him to walk exactly in the same path in which Christ walked on His way to God, and make that way to him *a new and living way*, with nothing of decay or weariness in his progress. This is the *fulness of faith* we are called to. But, above all, to look to Jesus in all the glory in which He has been revealed in the Epistle, as God and Man, as Leader and Forerunner, as Melchizedek, as the Minister of the sanctuary and Mediator of the new covenant—in one word, as *our great Priest over the house of God.* And, looking to Him, to claim that He shall do for us this one thing, to bring us nigh, and even on earth give us to dwell without a break in the presence of the Father.

Faith ever deals with impossibilities. Its only rule or measure is what God has said to be possible to Him. When we look at our lives and their failures, at our sinfulness and weakness, at those around us, the thought will come up— Is it for me? Dare I expect it? Is it not wearying myself in vain to think of it or to seek for it? Soul! the God who redeemed thee, when an enemy, with the blood of His Son—what thinkest thou? Would He not be willing thus to take thee to His heart? He who raised Jesus when He had died under the curse of thy sins, from the death of the grave to the throne of His glory, would He not be able to take thee too, and give thee a place within the veil? Do believe it. He longs to do it; He is able to do it. His home and His heart have room for thee even now. *Let us draw near in fulness of faith.*

In fulness of faith. The word has also reference to that full measure of faith which is found when the whole heart is filled and possessed by it. We have very little idea of how the weakness of our faith is owing to its being more a confident persuasion of the mind with regard to the truth of what God says, than the living apprehension and possession of the eternal spiritual realities of the truth with the heart. The Holy Spirit asks us first for a true heart, and then at once, as its first exercise, for *fulness of faith.* There is a faith of insight, a faith of desire, a faith of trust in the truth of the word, and a faith of personal acceptance. There is a faith of love that embraces, and a faith of will that holds fast, and a faith of sacrifice that gives up everything, and a faith of despair that abandons all hope in self, and a faith of rest that waits on God alone. This is all included in the faith of the true heart, the fulness of faith, in which the whole being surrenders and lets go all, and yields itself to God to do His work. *In fulness of faith let us draw near.*

In fulness of faith, not of thought. What God is about to do to you is supernatural, above what you can think. It is a love that passes knowledge that is going to take possession. God is the incomprehensible, the hidden One. The Holy Spirit is the secret, incomprehensible working and presence of God. Do not seek to understand everything. Draw nigh—it never says with a clear head, but with a true heart. Rest upon God to do for you far more than you understand in fulness of faith.

In fulness of faith, and not in fulness of feeling. When you come, and, gazing into the opened Holiest of All, hear the voice of Him that dwells between the cherubim call you to come in; and as you gaze—long, indeed—to enter and to dwell there, the word comes again, *Draw near with a true heart!* Your answer is, Yes, Lord; with my whole heart—with that new heart Thou Thyself hast given me. You make the surrender of yourself, to live only and always in His presence and for His service. The voice speaks again: Let it be Today—Now, *in fulness of faith.* You have accepted what He offers. You have given what He asks. You believe that He accepts the surrender. You believe that the great Priest over the house takes possession of your inner life, and brings you before God. And yet you wonder you feel so little changed. You feel just like the old self you were. Now is the time to listen to the voice—*In fulness of faith*, not of feeling! Look to God, who is able to do above what we ask or think. Trust His power. Look to Jesus on the throne, living there to bring you in. Claim the Spirit of the exalted One as His pentecostal gift. Remember these are all divine, spiritual mysteries of grace, to be revealed in you. Apart from feeling, without feeling, in fulness of faith, in bare, naked faith that honours God, enter in. Reckon yourself to be indeed alive to God in Christ Jesus, taken in into His presence, His love, His very heart.

1. Be followers of those who, through faith and longsuffering, inherited the promises. Faith accepts and rejoices in the gift; longsuffering waits for the full enjoyment; and so faith in due time inherits, and the promise becomes an experience. By faith at once take your place in the Holiest; wait on the Holy Spirit in your inner life to reveal it in the power of God; your High Priest will see to your inheriting the blessing.

2. In the fulness of the whole heart to accept the whole fulness of God's salvation—this is what God asks.

3. As in heaven, so on earth. The more I look at the fulness of grace in Christ, the more the fulness of faith will grow in me. Of His fulness have we received, and grace for grace.

4. A whole chapter is to be devoted to the exhibiting of what this fulness of faith implies. Let us go on to study it with the one object for which it is given—our entering into that life in the will and love of God which Jesus has secured for us.

7

Our Hearts Sprinkled

"Let us draw near... our hearts sprinkled from an evil conscience." (10:22)

In verse 19 we had *boldness through the blood of Jesus*, as one of the four precious things prepared for us by God. It is that actual liberty or right which the blood of Jesus gives, apart from any use we make of it. Along with the opened sanctuary, and the living way, and the great Priest, the blood and our boldness in it is a heavenly reality waiting our faith and acceptance. Here the blood is mentioned a second time, and our being sprinkled with it as one of the things God asks of us. It is in the personal application and experience of the power of the blood we are to draw nigh. The sense of the cleansing of the heart in the blood may be, must be, an unbroken consciousness; so shall we abide continually in God's presence. This second mention of the blood is in accord with what we had in Chapter 9 of its twofold sprinkling. First, Christ entered with it into heaven, to cleanse the heavenly things, and fulfil the type of the sprinkling on the mercy-seat. It proved its power with God in putting away sins. And then we read of its cleansing our conscience. The blood which has had its mighty operation in heaven itself has as mighty power in our hearts. It makes us partakers of a divine and eternal cleansing. In heaven the power of the blood is proved to be infinite and immeasurable, never-ceasing and eternal, giving boldness to enter even as Christ did. As the soul learns to believe and rejoice in this heavenly power of the blood, it will claim and receive the very same power in the heart; Jesus washes us in His blood, with a washing that is not at times or intervals, but, in the power of the endless life, a continuous experience, and we know by faith what it is to have, in a heavenly reality, *a heart sprinkled from an evil conscience.* We walk as those whose garments have been washed and made white. And grace is given, even for the life on earth, to keep our garments undefiled (Rev. 3:4).

There will ever be harmony between a home and those who dwell in it, between an environment and the life that is sustained by it. There must be harmony between the Holiest of All and the soul that is to enter in. That harmony begins with, and has its everlasting security in, the blood of sprinkling. The ever-living and never-ceasing energy of the blood, ever speaking better things than the blood of Abel, and keeping heaven open for me, has a like effect on my heart. The blood has put away the thought of sin from God; He remembers it no more for ever. The blood puts away the thought of sin in me too, taking away the evil conscience that condemns me. The better things which the blood speaks in heaven, it speaks in my heart too; it lifts me into that heavenly sphere, that new state of life and intercourse with God, in which an end has been made of sin, and the soul is taken in to the full and perfect enjoyment of the love of God.

The action of the blood in heaven is unceasing—never a moment but the blood is the delight of the Father and the song of the ransomed. Draw nigh when thou wilt, the blood is there, abiding continually; not a moment's interval. And even so will it be in the soul that enters in. The difficulty that staggers the faith of many lies just here; they cannot understand how one who has to live amid the cares and engagements and companionships of his daily life can every moment maintain a heart sprinkled from an evil conscience. They do not know that, if once, with a heart sprinkled, they enter in, they are in an inner sanctuary, where everything acts in the power of the upper world, in the power of an endless life. They breathe the inspiring, invigorating air of the Holiest of All; they breathe the Holy Spirit, and enjoy the power of the resurrection life. The Minister of the heavenly sanctuary is also the Mediator of the new covenant in our hearts. All He does in heaven He does each moment on earth in our heart, if faith will trust Him, for the blood of sprinkling is the blood of the covenant. The abiding continually is possible and sure, because He who is our High Priest abides continually.

And what may be the reason that so few Christians can testify of the joy and the power of a heart at all times sprinkled from an evil conscience? The answer is, That in the apprehension of this, as of every other truth, there are stages according to the measure of faith and faithfulness. See it in Israel. There you have three stages. The Israelite who entered the outer court saw the altar and the blood sprinkled there, and received such assurance of pardon as that could give him. The priest who was admitted to the Holy Place not only saw the blood sprinkled on the brazen altar, he had it sprinkled upon himself, and might see it sprinkled on the golden altar in the Holy Place. His contact with the blood was closer, and he was admitted to a nearer access. The access of the High Priest was still more complete; he might, with the blood for the mercy-seat, once a year enter within the veil. Even so there are outer-court Christians, who trust in Christ who died on Calvary, but know very little of His heavenly life, or near access to God, or service for others. Beyond these there are Christians who know that they are called to be priests, and to live in the service of God and their fellow-men. They know more of the power of the blood as setting apart for service; but yet their life is still without the veil. But then come those who know what Christ's entering with His blood implies and procures, and who experience that the Holy Spirit applies the blood in such power, that it indeed brings to the life in the inner sanctuary, in the full and abiding joy of God's presence.*

Let us draw near, with a true heart, in fulness of faith, having our hearts sprinkled from an evil conscience. Oh, let us not bring reproach upon the blood of the Lamb by

---

*"The blood contains life (John 6:63). The blood not only removes death (judicial and spiritual), but it gives and preserves life (judicial and spiritual). It quickens. We are not only to be sprinkled with it outwardly, but we are to receive it inwardly, to drink it. As with the water, so with the blood. They are for inward as well as outward application."—H. Bonar. And because the twofold application is essentially one, the sprinkling is in a power that purifies and quickens the whole inner life.

not believing in its power to give us perfect access to God. Let us listen and hear them sing without ceasing the praise of the blood of the Lamb in heaven; as we trust and honour and rejoice in it, we shall enter the heaven of God's presence.

1. "Wherein is the blood of Jesus better than the blood of goats and bulls, if it cannot free us from the spirit of bondage and the evil conscience, if it cannot give us a full glad confidence before God? What Jesus hath perfected, we can experience and enjoy as perfect in our heart and conscience. You dishonour your Saviour when you do not seek to experience that He has perfected you as touching the conscience, and when you do not live with a heart entirely cleansed from the evil conscience."—Steinhofer.

2. *A true heart*—a heart sprinkled: you see everything depends upon the heart. God can do nothing for us from without, only by what He can put into the heart. Of all that Jesus is and does as High Priest in heaven I cannot have the least experience, but as it is revealed in the heart. The whole work of the Holy Spirit is in the heart. Let us draw nigh with a true heart, a sprinkled heart, our inmost being under the heavenly power of the blood, entirely and unceasingly.

8

Our Body Washed

"Let us draw near... our body washed
with pure water." (10:22)

Man belongs to two worlds, the visible and the invisible. In his constitution, the material and the spiritual, body and soul, are wonderfully united. In the fall both came under the power of sin and death; in redemption deliverance has been provided for both. It is not only in the interior life of the soul, but in that of the body too, that the power of redemption can be manifested.

In the Old Testament worship, the external was the more prominent. It consisted mostly in carnal ordinances, imposed until a time of reformation. They taught a measure of truth, they exercised a certain influence on the heart, but they could not make the worshipper perfect. It was only with the New Testament that the religion of the inner life, the worship of God in spirit and truth, was revealed. And yet we need to be on the watch lest the pursuit of the inner life lead us to neglect the external. It is in the body, as much as in the spirit, that the saving power of Christ Jesus must be felt. It was with this view that our Lord adopted one of the Jewish washings, and instituted

OUR BODY WASHED 37

the baptism with water. He that believed with the heart, came with the body to be baptized. It was a token that the whole exterior physical life, with all its functions and powers, was to be His too. It was in this connection John wrote: *There are three who bear witness, the Spirit and the water and the blood.* The same Spirit who applies the blood in power to the heart, takes possession and mastery of the body washed with water. And where in Scripture the word and water are joined together (Eph. 5:26; John 13:10; 15:3), it is because the word is the external manifestation of what must rule our whole outer life too.*

It is in this connection the two expressions are used here: *Our hearts sprinkled from an evil conscience, our body washed with pure water.* The thought was suggested to our author by the service of the tabernacle. In the court there were only two things to be seen— the brazen altar and the laver. At the one, the priest received and sprinkled the blood; at the other, he found the water in which he washed, ere he entered the Holy Place. At the installation of the priests in their office, they were first washed and then sprinkled with blood (Ex. 29:4, 20). On the great day of atonement, the high priest, too, had first to wash ere he entered into the Holiest with the blood (Lev. 16:4). And so the lesson comes to us that if we draw near with *hearts sprinkled from an evil conscience*, we must also have *the body washed with pure water.* The liberty of ac-

---

*Eph. 5:26: "...the washing of water with the word." The word of God is portrayed by water, and our daily actions portrayed by our bodies. As we read the word and submit to it, our actions are washed by the word and we stay clean from sin, just like our body being washed with water.

cess, the cleansing the blood gives, can only be enjoyed in a life of which every action is cleansed by the word. Not only in the heart and the disposition, but in the body and the outer visible life, everything must be clean. *Who shall ascend into the hill of the Lord? or who shall stand in His Holy Place? He that hath clean hands, and a pure heart.* A heart sprinkled with the blood, a body washed with pure water from every stain,—these God hath joined together; let no man separate them. There have been some who have sought very earnestly to enter into the Holiest of All and have failed. The reason was that they had not clean hands, they were not ready to have everything that is not perfectly holy, discovered and put away. Cleanse your hands, ye sinners, and purify your hearts, ye double-minded—is a word that always holds. The blood of Christ has unspeakable and everlasting power for the soul that, with a true heart, is ready to put away every sin. Where this is not the case, and the body is not washed with pure water, the perfect conscience which the blood gives cannot be enjoyed.

Our body washed with pure water. It is not only in spirit, but with the body too, we enter into the Holiest of All. It is on us here, where we are in the body, that the presence of God descends. Our whole life in the flesh is to be in that presence; the body is very specially the temple, and in charge of the Holy Spirit; in the body the Father is to be glorified. Our whole being, body, soul, and spirit, is, in the power of the Holy Spirit, a holy sacrifice upon the altar, a living sacrifice for service before God. With the body, too, we live and walk in the Holiest. Our eating and drinking, our sleeping, our clothing, our labour and relaxation,—all these things have more influence on our spiritual life than we know. They often interrupt and break the fellowship we seek to maintain. The heart and the body are inseparably joined; a heart sprinkled from an evil conscience needs a body washed with pure water.

When He cometh into the world, He saith, A body didst thou prepare for Me. This word of Christ must be adopted by each of His followers. Nothing will help us to live in this world, and keep ourselves unspotted, but the Spirit that was in Christ, that looked upon His body as prepared by God for His service; that looks upon our body as prepared by Him too, that we might offer it to Him. Like Christ, we too have a body, in which the Holy Spirit dwells. Like Christ, we too must yield our body, with every member, every power, every action, to fulfil His will, to be offered up to Him, to glorify Him. Like Christ, we must prove in our body that we are holy to the Lord.

The blood that is sprinkled on thy heart came from the body of Jesus, prepared by God, and, in His whole life, even to His one offering, given up to God. The object of that blood sprinkling is that thy body, of which the heart sprinkled with the blood is the life, should, like His, be wholly given up to God, should be in all thy walk a body washed with pure water. Oh, seek to take in this blessed truth, and to accept it fully. The heart sprinkled with the blood points to the divine side of redemption, the body washed with pure water, to the human side. Let faith in the divine cleansing and obedience to the call for us to cleanse ourselves be closely linked together. God's work and thy work will be truly one. The heart sprinkled from the evil conscience will then become an unbroken experience, and the blood of the Lamb, the ever-living motive and power for a life in the body, like Christ's, a sacrifice holy and acceptable to God.

1. I am deeply persuaded that in the self-pleasing which we allow in gratifying the claims of the body, we shall find one of the most frequent causes of the gradual decline of our fellowship with God. Do remember, it was through the body that Satan conquered in Paradise; it was in the body he tempted Christ and had to be resisted. It was in suffering of the body, as when He hungered, that Christ was perfected. It is only when the law of self-denial is strictly applied to the body, that we can dwell in the Holiest.

2. He was tempted in all points, like as we are—in His body very specially, and is able to succour us. Let the committal of our body into the keeping and the rule of Jesus be very definite and entire.

3. "If Miranda was to run a race for her life, she would submit to a diet that was proper for it. As the race which is set before her is a race for holiness and heavenly affection, so her everyday diet has only this one end—to make her body fitter for this spiritual life."

9

Let Us Draw Near

"Therefore, brethren... let us draw near."
(10:19, 22)

We have studied the four great blessings of the new worship, as the motives and encouragements for us to draw nigh. They are—*the Holiest opened up, Boldness through the blood, the New and living way,* and the *Great Priest over the house of God.* And we have considered the four great marks of the true worshipper—*A true heart, Fulness of faith, The heart sprinkled,* and *The body cleansed.* We now come to the four injunctions which come to us out of the opened sanctuary—and specially to the first—*Let us draw near.* Both in speaking of the entering in of Christ, and the power of His blood in Chapter 9, and in the exposition of our context, we have had abundant occasion to point out what is meant by this entering in, and what is needed for it. And yet it may be well to gather up all we have said, and in the very simplest way possible, once again, by the grace of God, to throw open the door, and to help each honest-hearted child of God to enter in, and take his place for life, in the home the Father has prepared for him.

And first of all I would say: *Believe that a life in the Holiest of All, a life of continual abiding in God's presence, is most certainly your duty and within your power.* As long as this appears a vague uncertainty, the study of our Epistle must be in vain. Its whole teaching has been to prove that the wonderful priesthood of Christ, in which He does everything *in the power of an endless life, and is therefore able to save completely*; that His having opened a way through the rent veil into the Holiest, and entered in with His blood; that His sitting on the throne in heavenly power, as Minister of the sanctuary and Mediator of the covenant; that all this means nothing if it does not mean—*the Holiest is open for us.* We may, we must, and we can live there. What is the meaning of this summing up of all, *Wherefore, brethren, having boldness to enter— let us draw near*, if a real entrance into and abode in the Holiest is not for us? No, beloved Christian, do believe, it can be. Say: *God really means me to enter and dwell, and spend my whole life, in the conscious enjoyment of His immediate presence.* Let no thought of thy weakness and unfaithfulness hold thee back. Begin to look at God, who has set the door open and calls thee in; at the blood that has prevailed over sin and death, and given thee a boldness that nothing can hinder; at Christ the almighty and most loving High Priest, who is to bring thee in and keep thee in; and believe: Yes, such a life is meant for me; it is possible; it is my duty; God calls me to it; and say then, whether thy heart would not desire and long to enter into this blessed rest, the home of God's love.

The second step is the surrender to Christ, by Him to be brought into this life of abiding fellowship with God.

This surrender implies an entire giving up of the life of nature and of self; an entire separation from the world and its spirit; an entire death to my own will, and acceptance of God's will to command my life, in all things, down to the very least. To some this surrender comes as the being convicted of a number of things which they thought harmless, and which they now see to have been in the will of the flesh and of man. To others it comes as a call to part with some single doubtful thing, or some sin against which they have hopelessly struggled. The surrender of all becomes only possible when the soul sees how truly and entirely Jesus, the Mediator of the new covenant, has undertaken for all, and engages to put His own delight in God's law into the heart, to give the will and the strength to live in all God's will. That faith gives the courage to place oneself before Christ and to say —Lord, here am I, ready to be led by Thee in the new and living way of death to my will, and a life in God's will alone: I give up all to Thee.

Then comes, accompanying this surrender, *the faith that Jesus does now accept and undertake for all.* The more general faith in His power, which led to the surrender, becomes a personal appropriation. I know that I cannot lift or force myself into the Holiest. I trust Jesus, as my almighty and ever-living Priest on the throne, even now, at this moment, to take me in within the veil, to take charge of me there, and enable me to walk up and down before the face of the living God, and serve Him. However high and impossible such a life appears, I cannot doubt but that He who with His blood opened the Holiest for me will take me in; and that He who sits on the throne as my great

High Priest is able and faithful to keep me in God's presence. Apart from any feeling or experience of a change, I believe He takes me in, and I say: Thank God, I am in the Holiest. *Let us draw near in fulness of faith.*

And then follows, *the life of faith in the Holiest*, holding fast my confidence and the glorying of hope firm to the end. I believe Jesus takes me in to the fulfilment and the experience of all the new covenant blessings, and makes me inherit all the promises. I look to Him day by day to seal my faith with the Holy Ghost sent down from heaven in my heart. The disciples, when their Lord ascended the throne, kept waiting, praising, praying, till the Spirit came as the witness and the revealer within their hearts of the glory of Jesus at the right hand of God. It was on the day of Pentecost that they truly entered within the veil, to which the Forerunner had drawn their longing hearts. They entered upon a state of life in which they were dead to their own will, and alive to God's will; in which Christ dwelling in their hearts by the Holy Spirit kept them in the presence and love of God. In this state of life we too can be kept. As sure as Christ Jesus is wholly ours, each one of us is called to live in the full enjoyment of the pentecostal blessing. The soul that gives itself over to a life within the veil, in full surrender and in simple faith, can count upon this most surely, that, in the power of the eternal, the pentecostal Spirit in the heart, faith will become experience, and the joy unspeakable be its abiding portion. *Wherefore, brethren, let us draw near!*

1. *Having boldness to enter in* is the summary of the doctrinal teaching of the first half of the Epistle; *let us draw*

nigh, the summary of my life and practice which the second half expounds.

2. The faith that appropriates the blessing—Jesus now takes me in and gives me my place and my life in the Father's presence—is but a beginning. Faith must now count upon the Holy Spirit, in His pentecostal power, bringing down the kingdom of heaven to us, to make it a personal experience. Until this comes, faith must in patience wait till it obtains the promise. In accordance with the teaching we have: "Cast not away therefore your boldness. For ye have need of patience, that, having done the will of God, ye may receive the promise" (Heb. 10:35, 36).

10

Let Us Hold Fast the Confession of Our Hope

"Let us hold fast the confession of our hope that it waver not; for He is faithful that promised."
(10:23)

The three chief words of this injunction we have had before—*Hold fast, Confession, Hope.* If we *hold fast* the glorying of our *hope* firm to the end. Give diligence to *the fulness of hope.* Christ the *High Priest of our profession.* Let us *hold fast* our *confession.* A *better hope*, by which we draw nigh to God. We have now been brought to see what Christian perfection is, in that perfect life in God's presence to which Jesus brings us in: here, more than ever, we shall need to hold fast our hope.

Faith and hope ever go together. "*Faith* is the substance of things *hoped* for." Faith accepts the promise in its divine reality, hope goes forward to examine and picture and rejoice in the treasures which faith has accepted. And so here, on the words, *Let us draw near in fulness of faith*, there follows immediately, *Let us hold fast the confession of our hope.* Life in the Holiest, in the nearness of God, must be characterised by an infinite hopefulness.

It is not difficult to see the reason of this. Entering into the Holiest is only the beginning of the true Christian life. As we tarry there, God can begin to do His work of grace in power. There the holiness of God can overshadow us, and can be assimilated into our life and character. There we can learn to worship in that true humility and meekness and resignation to God's will, which does not come at once, but in which we may grow up even as Jesus did. There we have to learn the holy art of intercession, so as to pray the prayer that prevails. There we wait to receive in larger measure, in ever fresh communications, that fulness of the Spirit which comes and is maintained only by close and living contact with Jesus on the throne. The entrance into the Holiest is only a beginning. It is to be a life in which we every hour receive everything from God, in which God's working is to be all in all. Here, if anywhere, we have need of an infinite hopefulness. After we have entered in, we shall very probably not find what we expected. The light and the joy and the power may not come at once. Within the veil it is still, nay rather, it is eminently, a life of faith, not looking to ourselves, but to God, and hoping in Him. Faith will still be tried, will perhaps most be tried, when God wants most to bless. Hope is the daughter of faith, the messenger it sends out to see what is to come: it is hope that becomes the strength and support of faith. Here, in the Holiest, let us above all hold fast our confidence and the glorying of our hope firm unto the end. Let us rejoice in hope of the glory of God, as it will most surely be revealed in our souls.

Let us hold fast the confession of our hope. Men always speak out of the abundance of the heart of that which they hope for. We, too, must confess and give expression to our hope. The confession strengthens the hope; what we utter becomes clearer and more real to us. It glorifies God. It helps and encourages those around us. It makes God, and men, and ourselves, see that we are committed to it. Let us hold fast the confession of our hope, that it waver not. Let the better hope by which we draw nigh to God, by which we enter within the veil, be the one thing we hold fast and confess with a confidence that never wavers. Let the blessed hope of being kept day by day in God's love, the hope of a continual abiding in Jesus and where He is, in the light of God, be our anchor within the veil.

For He is faithful that promised. Study the references on the word "promise" in this Epistle, and see what a large place they take in God's dealings with His people, and learn how much your life depends on your relation to the promises. Connect the promises, as is here done, with the promiser; connect the promiser with His unchanging faithfulness as God, and your hope will become a glorying in God, through Jesus Christ our Lord. *Faithful is He that promised*: that word lies at the root of the life within the veil. Just as it is God who speaks in Christ, who sent Him, who appointed Him Priest, who perfected Him, so it is God to whom Christ brings us into the Holiest for Him now to work directly and continually in us that life in which, as His redeemed creatures, we are to live. This is the blessedness of being brought into the Holiest: Christ has brought us *to God.* And we are now in the right place and spirit for honouring Him as God—that is, for allowing Him to work freely, immediately, unceasingly in us such a life as He wrought in Christ. He is faithful that promised. God is going to fulfil His promises of life and love, of blessing and fruitfulness, in a way we have no conception of. *Let us hold fast the confession of our hope, for He is faithful that promised.*

My reader, thou hast heard the call, *Let us draw near in fulness of faith.* And hast obeyed? And hast believed that Jesus takes thee into a life of abiding in God's presence? And art, even amid the absence of feeling or experience, even amid the doubts and fears that threaten to press in, holding fast the confession of thy hope?—Listen, look up—*He is faithful that promised!* Let this be thy rock. Say continually—*O my soul, hope thou in God, for I shall yet praise Him. Thou art my hope, O God! I will hope continually, and praise Thee yet more and more.* This is the blessing of the inner sanctuary, that thou hast found thy true place at God's feet, there to wait in absolute dependence and helplessness on His working. Look up in the boldness the blood gives thee. Look up with a true heart, in which the Holy Spirit dwells and works. Look up with a heart sprinkled by thy blessed High Priest with the blood—and hope, yes hope in God, to do His divine work in thy soul. Let Him be to thee more than ever the God of hope. Claim the fulfilment of the promise of His word: *The God of hope fill you with all joy and peace in believing, that ye may abound in hope, in the power of the Holy Ghost.* The infinite faithful God, as the God of our hope, filling us with joy and peace in believing, and we learning to abound in hope through the power of the Holy Ghost: Be this our life in the secret of God's presence!

1. Fulness of faith and fulness of hope are two dispositions that mark the true heart. It is because we are to have

nothing in ourselves, and God is to be all and to do all, that our whole attitude is to be looking up to Him, expecting and receiving what He is to do.

2. *That ye may abound in hope, through the power of the Holy Ghost.* See how the life in the Holiest depends entirely upon the Holy Spirit dwelling within us. For this life we need to *be filled with the Spirit*, to have the immediate, continual moving of the Spirit. Not a moment can we dwell in the Holiest but by the Holy Spirit. Not a moment but we can dwell in the Holiest by the Holy Spirit. Let us abound in this hope, through the power of the Holy Spirit.

11

Let Us Provoke unto Love

"And let us consider one another, to provoke
unto love and good works." (10:24)

We have had the *fulness of faith* in which we are to draw nigh, and the *confession of hope* we are to hold fast; now follows the third of the sister graces: *Let us consider one another*—let us prove our love and care for each other in the effort—*to provoke unto love and good works.* These three thoughts form the subdivisions of the practical part of the Epistle. Chapter 11 may well be headed, *The fulness of faith*; Chapter 12:1–14, *The patience of hope*; and Chapter 13, *Love and good works.*

And let us consider one another. He that enters into the Holiest enters into the home of eternal love; the air he breathes there is love; the highest blessing he can receive there is a heart in which the love of God is shed abroad in power by the Holy Ghost, and which is on the path to be made perfect in love. *That thou mayest know how thou oughtest to behave thyself in the house of God*—remember this, *Faith and hope shall pass away, but love abideth ever. The chief of these is love.*

Let us consider one another. When first we seek the entrance into the Holiest, the thought is mostly of ourselves. And when we have entered in in faith, it is as if it is all we can do to stand before God, and wait on Him for what He has promised to do for us. But it is not long before we perceive that the Holiest and the Lamb are not for us alone; that there are others within with whom it is blessed to have fellowship in praising God; that there are some without who need our help to be brought in. It is into the love of God that we have had access given us; that love enters our hearts; and we see ourselves called to live like Christ in entire devotion to those around us.

Let us consider one another. All the redeemed form one body. Each one is dependent on the other, each one is for the welfare of the other. Let us beware of the self-deception that thinks it possible to enter the Holiest, into the nearest intercourse with God, in the spirit of selfishness. It cannot be. The new and living way Jesus opened up is the way of self-sacrificing love. The entrance into the Holiest is given to us as priests, there to be filled with the Spirit and the love of Christ, and to go out and bring God's blessing to others.

Let us consider one another. The same Spirit that said, *Consider Christ Jesus*—take time, and give attention to know Him well—says to us, *Consider one another*— take time, and give attention to know the needs of your brethren around you. How many are there whose circumstances are so unfavourable, whose knowledge is so limited, whose whole life is so hopeless, that there is but little prospect of their ever attaining the better life. For them there is but one thing to be done: *We that are strong ought to bear the infirmities of the weak, and not to please ourselves* (Rom.

15:1). Each one who begins to see what the blessedness is of a life in the full surrender to Christ, should offer himself to Christ, to be made His messenger to the feeble and the weary.

Consider one another, to provoke unto love and good works.—Love and good works: These are to be the aim of the Church in the exercise of its fellowship. Everything that can hinder love is to be sacrificed and set aside. Everything that can promote, and prove, and provoke others to, love is to be studied and performed. And with love good works too. The Church has been redeemed by Christ, to prove to the world what power He has to cleanse from sin, to conquer evil, to restore to holiness and to goodness. Let us consider one another, in every possible way, to provoke, to stir up, to help to love and good works.

The chief thought is this: Life in the Holiest must be a life of love. As earnest as the injunction, *Let us draw nigh* in fulness of faith, *Let us hold fast* the confession of our hope, is this: *Let us consider one another* to provoke unto love and good works. God is love. And all He has done for us in His Son, as revealed in this Epistle, is love. And Christ is love. And there can be no real access to God as a union with Him in His holy will, no real communion with Him, but in the Spirit of love. Our entering into the Holiest is mere imagination if we do not yield ourselves to the love of God in Christ, to be filled and used for the welfare and joy of our fellow-men.

O Christian! study what love is. Study it in the word, in Christ, in God. As thou seest Him to be an ever-flowing fountain of all goodness, who has His very being and glory in this, that He lives in all that exists, and communicates to all His own blessedness and perfection as far as they are capable of it, thou wilt learn to acknowledge that he that loveth not hath not known God. And thou wilt learn, too, to admit more deeply and truly than ever before, that no effort of thy will can bring forth love; it must be given thee from above. This will become to thee one of the chief joys and beauties of the Holiest of All, that there thou canst wait on the God of love to fill thee with His love. God hath the power to shed abroad His love in our hearts, by the Holy Spirit given unto us. He has promised to give Christ so dwelling in our heart by faith, that we shall be rooted and grounded in love, and know and have in us something of a love that passeth knowledge. The very atmosphere of the Holiest is love. Just as I breathe in the air in which I live, so the soul that abides in the presence of God breathes the air of the upper world. The promise held out to us, and the hour of its fulfilment, will come, when the love of God will be perfected in us, and we are made perfect in love. Nowhere can this be but in the Holiest; but there most surely. Let us draw nigh in the fulness of faith, and consider one another. While we are only thinking of others to bring God's love to them, we shall find God thinking of us, and filling us with it.

What a difference it would make in the world if every believer were to give himself with his whole heart to live for his fellow-men! What a difference to his own life, as he yielded himself to God's saving love in its striving for souls! What a difference to all our Christian agencies, suffering for want of devoted, whole-hearted helpers! What a difference to our churches, as they rose to know what they have been gathered for! What a difference to thousands of lost ones, who would learn with wonder what love there is in God's children, what power and blessing in that love! Let us consider one another.

1. It is the very essence, the beauty, and the glory of the salvation of Christ, that it is for all. He that truly receives it, as the Holy Spirit gives it, receives it as a salvation for all, and feels himself impelled to communicate it to others. The baptism of fire is a baptism of redeeming love, but that not as a mere emotion, but a power at once to consider and to care for others.

2. How impossible to love others and give all for them in our strength! This is one of the real gifts to be waited for in the Holiest of All, to be received in the power of the Pentecostal Spirit—the love of God so shed abroad in the heart, that we spontaneously, unceasingly, joyfully love, because it is our very nature.

12

The Assembling Together

> "Not forsaking the assembling of ourselves together, as the custom of some is, but exhorting one another; and so much the more, as ye see the day drawing nigh." (10:25)

The inward and the outward must ever go together. As there is in every man a hidden inner life of the soul, along with the outer life of the body, so too in the Church of Christ. All its members are one body; the inward unity must be proved in active exercise, it must be seen in the assembling together. The assembling of His saints has its ground in a divine appointment as well as in the very nature of things; all who have entered into the Holiest to meet their God must turn to the meeting of His people. The tabernacle of old was the tent of meeting; to meet God and to meet our fellow-men are equally needful. Among the Hebrews it was already the custom with some to forsake the assembling together; it was one of the dangerous symptoms of backsliding. They are reminded, not only of the personal duty of each to be faithful, but also to care for others, and to exhort one another. For the exercise and strengthening of the faith and hope and love, to which we have just been urged; for the full development of the life in the Holiest of All; for the helping and comforting of all who are feeble; for the cultivation of the fellowship of the Spirit and the Word—the assembling of ourselves together has unspeakable value. Let us listen to the exhortation, in connection with our entrance into the Holiest: *Not forsaking the assembling of ourselves together, as the custom of some is.*

If we would rightly apprehend the import of this word, let us not forget the link to its context. Our section has been teaching us what life in the Holiest is to be. As those who have drawn near to God, we are to draw near to our fellow-men. Meeting God is a thing of infinite blessedness and peace and power. Meeting our fellow-men is often accompanied with so much of weakness, distraction, and failure, that some have thought it indeed better to forsake the assembling together. Let us see how life in the Holiest of All points to both the duty and the power of our assemblies.

It suggests the duty. The Holiest of All is the home of eternal love. It is love dwells there. It is love that came forth from there to seek me and bring me in. It is into the everlasting love I have been welcomed and taken in. It is love that has been shed abroad in my heart. My entrance in was only in the path of self-sacrifice; my abiding there can only be as one dead to self and filled with love. And love seeketh not its own; it gives itself away, and only lives to make others partakers of its happiness. And it loves the assembly of God's people, not only for what it needs and hopes to receive, but for the communion of saints, and the help it can give in helping and encouraging others.

It not only does this, but obeys the added injunction—

Exhorting one another. It seeks to watch over those who are in danger of becoming unfaithful. It cares for those who have grown careless in their neglect. True love is quick of invention; it devises means for making smaller or nearer or more attractive assemblies for those who have become estranged. It counts nothing too humble or too difficult, if it may but win back to the gathering of God's children those who may there be blessed and saved. It lives in the Holiest of God's love; it gives itself up to the one work of winning others to know that love.

The life in the Holiest is thus not only the motive, but the power for doing the work aright. Yes, it is as those who profess to have entered the Holiest of All truly draw near to God, and prove the power of fellowship with Him, that they will have power in prayer and speech and service among their fellow-Christians. The Holiest of All is the place for daily worship and consecration and intercession; even a little band in the assembly will have power to make the divine presence felt. The worship in the place of prayer may become so linked to the secret worship of the Holiest of All, that its blessing may come to others who have never known of it. God is willing so to bless the fellowship of His redeemed, that the assembly shall be crowned with a fuller sense of His love and presence, than ever can be found in the solitary approach to Him. *Wherefore, brethren, having boldness to enter into the Holiest, let us draw near; not forsaking the assembly of ourselves together, but exhorting one another.*

And so much the more as ye see the day approaching. The writer has doubtless in view the then approaching day of judgment on Jerusalem. We know not in how far the perspective of prophecy was clearly revealed, and that day was connected with the coming of the Lord Himself. It is enough for us to know that the fear of an approaching day of judgment was the motive to which appeal is made; and that not only to move the indifferent, but specially to urge the earnest to exhort others. Christians need to be reminded of the terrible doom hanging over the world, and of all the solemn eternal realities connected with our Lord's coming in their bearing upon our daily life. So will our efforts for helping and saving others all be under the power of the thought of how short the time is, how terrible the fate of those who perish, and how urgent the call for everyone who knows redeeming love to do its work with all his might. In the Holiest of All we hear the voice of warning, and come out to save ere it be too late.

1. Note the intensely practical character of the gospel. Our section (19–25) is only one sentence. It begins with spiritual, heavenly mysteries; it ends in the plainest rules for our conduct to our fellow-men. Let us be sure that the deeper we enter into the perfection-teaching of Chapter 7–10, the fitter we shall be to be a blessing in the world.

2. When Christ spoke His farewell discourse to His disciples, one of the things He pressed most urgently was that they should love one another. He loves all His redeemed ones, however feeble or perverse they be, so intently, that He tells us that we cannot prove our real love to Him in any other way than by loving them; the proof of a real entrance into the Holiest of All is the humility and gentleness and self-sacrifice with which we speak and think and prove our care of one another.

3. Study carefully the connection between these last twelve meditations, and seek to get a clear hold of the unity of thought in this portion, the living centre of the Epistle.

Conclusion

There are some of God's children who have read this book, to whom the teaching it contains may appear new or strange, and who, for this reason, may not fully have taken in the one lesson from God's word it has sought to bring. There may be others who have accepted the teaching, and admit its truth, and yet by reason of unbelief or lack of whole-heartedness, have not entered into the blessed life to which this portion of God's word has opened the gate so wide. For the sake of such, I feel urged once again to give a simple summary of the truth the word has taught us, to trace with them the steps of the Christian life as it has marked them out, and to beseech them to see at what point it is they have failed. Do believe, my dear brother or sister, that it is in very deed the will of God that you should enter into the Holiest, and live there. Rest not till, step by step, you have at every point yielded yourself to God's command: you may trust Him to make all the salvation He has prepared in Christ, your own blessed possession and experience.

1. The Holiest is opened now. Full access into God's presence is secured to us. A continuous and unbroken experience of God's presence every day is a possibility, is a certainty. We are called to enter in and live there with Jesus. This is the consummation of His work as High Priest, to bring us in, and keep us there. Nothing in heaven, or earth, or hell, can prevent you entering in and abiding here continually and for ever, if you are willing.

Do not satisfy yourself with the thought that there are many Christians who have never entered in. Look up to the Father calling you in. Humble yourself under the thought: My Father has prepared this home for me. His love longs to have me live with Him all the day. I have refused to believe that it can be, and, instead of His immediate nearness and continual fellowship, live at a distance. Oh, do count it a settled thing: the Holiest is opened for us to enter in and dwell with Jesus, and say to God that you will not rest till it is your experience.

2. We have boldness through the blood. Is not this what has kept you back? You have never taken time to study, to believe, to realise the infinite worth and power of the blood of the Son of God. It conquered sin, and death, and hell. It opened heaven to Jesus our Surety. It will most surely bring you in; it will remove all the fear and doubt your sin and impotence can cause; it will enable you with the utmost confidence and boldness to draw nigh and claim admittance. See to it, O child of God, that you honour the blood, that you glory in its power; it can bring you in.

3. A new and living way has been dedicated for us. Are you willing to enter upon this way. To the flesh it appears hard and impossible. It is the way in which Christ walked; the way of self-sacrifice; the way of entire surrender to God's will; the way of death to self and the world; of being humbled and made obedient unto death. You surely would not wish or expect to enter heaven in any other way than Christ did, in any other way than the will of God. Give up at once the half-hearted religion that fears an entire consecration to the most blessed will of God:

give yourself at once wholly to it; choose and enter even now upon the new way.

It is a living way. The Holy Spirit lives and moves in it, and bears all who walk in it. Give up yourself to the Blessed Jesus to follow Him in it: in His strength it will be to you the highway of peace and holiness.

4. We have Jesus as our Priest over the House of God. Have you not learnt from the Epistle that the one work of Jesus as our High Priest is to bring us nigh to God? So nigh that in actual life and experience we can know and enjoy His nearness all the day? Is He not Priest over the House of God, the Father's Home, just to bring us in and watch over us there, and by His dwelling in us, to make us one with Himself, living our life in the immediate presence of the Father?

Oh, beloved, will you not begin to trust Jesus for this, His heart's desire, and yield yourself to enter in?

5. God asks a true heart. And that you have. He has given you a new heart. And the new heart is a true heart. Believe it, and act upon it. Believe in the power of the Spirit within you to act it out: come at once and say that with your whole heart, with a true heart, you desire to enter in. Look not at sin within, or at feelings: come in the faith of what God has said, of the new nature He has given you, and enter with a true heart. Choose, resolve, will, to say to Jesus that you cannot longer stand without; that you are ready, in the boldness the precious blood gives, to draw nigh and abide with Him.

6. God calls you to come in fulness of faith. And God never asks for faith, without giving a sure ground and abundant reason for it. And if you will but look up to Him, and what He has done in giving His Son to be your

High Priest, and the blood of His Son to be your confidence; in opening the Holiest for you; in giving the Holy Spirit to lead you in the living way of union with Jesus—surely you cannot doubt or fear. No, at once begin and say: Whatever may appear dark or difficult, of this I am confident: my weakness cannot hinder me: I trust God, I trust Jesus, I trust the Blood, I trust the Holy Spirit: I shall surely enter in.

7. Let the heart be sprinkled with the blood. We have seen the boldness the blood gives; we have heard the call to come with the true heart. Let the two be inseparably united. The blood is the sign that Jesus gave Himself wholly, His very life: let the true heart give itself wholly to trust and yield to the blood. The power of the blood is, it opened heaven and dwells there for ever: be sure, thine heart, sprinkled with the blood, rises into the heaven of God's love. Begin now and sing daily the song: "To Him that loved us, and washed us from our sins in His blood." The power of the blood, if thou wilt give thy whole heart up to it, will bring heaven and its joy, the joy of God's presence, down into thee.

8. Let the body be washed with pure water. Surely, in sight of all the wonderful privilege just set before us, there needs no further pleading to make you willing to put away every sin, every habit, every indulgence of the body, that interferes with full and abiding communion with God. Think ever of what Christ is doing—keeping the heart, by the power of the Holy Spirit, sprinkled with His blood in its heavenly sanctifying power—and let that urge you to put away and cleanse yourself from everything, the greatest or the least, that could hinder you dwelling in the Holiest. Wait on God in prayer till His presence be the power that rules the whole being.

9. Let us draw near. That is, let us enter in, and appear before God. Yes, let each one of us, with his whole heart, with his whole life and walk, draw near, and abide in the blessed nearness of God.

This is the sum and substance of the gospel. This is what Christ can give, because He is able to save completely. This, alas! is what many Christians do not possess, do not even seek, do not even know of. My reader! I beseech you, be not content with anything less than this—a life every moment in the presence of God, through the mighty keeping power of Jesus. His one work is to bring us near to God: yield yourself to Him for it. He will do it. Let us draw near.

10. Let us hold fast the confession of our hope. Lift up your heart above all fears, and doubts, and evil forebodings of unbelief as to failure, and hope against hope. Abound in hope. Confess your hope. Speak it out to God and your fellow-believer, that you have set your hope upon God for a life of ever-increasing nearness of fellowship with Him. Hold fast the confession of the hope firm to the end, with the one thought: He is faithful that promised. Live through any failure or disappointment that may come in the hope of what God will do, and you will find that hope maketh not ashamed. A life in the Holiest of All is your heritage.

11. Let us live in love. The Holiest of All is the home of God's love. The new and living way is the way of death to self and self-will. The Great Priest over the House of God, Jesus, can bring you nigh in no other way than by entering into you, becoming your life, animating you with His Spirit and disposition. Believe in Him for this. And Jesus is the Son of God's love, born of that love, filled with it, its messenger and dispenser. Yield yourself to the love of Christ, who pleased not Himself: walk in love as He loved us. Give yourself to a life of love, considering one another, provoking to love and good works. In the power of Jesus, abiding continually in the life of love, in the love and presence of God, is possible.

12. Let us maintain the communion of the saints. Let love manifest itself as a unity of the body, a binding together of the members in external fellowship and intercourse. Let us remember the Spirit of Christ is not given to us in isolation and separation from each other. As we live in the Holiest of All, we shall learn how closely we are one with each member of Christ; how our own life in God's love depends upon our relation to our brethren; how their life and growth must be our care, and will be our reward. A life in the Holiest of God's presence will be a life of love and labour, of power and blessing.

Beloved reader, have you in very deed accepted the teaching of God's word, that the Father calls you to dwell in the Holiest of all? Have you entered in? If not, I pray you, in the name of our great High Priest, who waits to bring you in, rest not till you have drawn nigh, and found your abiding-place in the secret of God's presence.

RHP Essential Classics

T. AUSTIN-SPARKS
   The School of Christ
   The inner working of the Holy Spirit

E. M. BOUNDS
   Power Through Prayer
   A stirring exhortation to pray

JOHN BUNYAN
   The Holy War
   Bunyan's other great masterpiece
   The Pilgrim's Progress
   The classic allegory of the Christian life

CHARLES FINNEY
   Revival
   God's way of revival

A. P. FITT
   D. L. Moody
   The life of the great evangelist

ROY HESSION
   The Calvary Road
   The way of personal revival
   Our Nearest Kinsman
   The message of hope from the book of Ruth
   Not I, But Christ
   The Christian's relationship with Jesus from the life of David
   The Power of God's Grace
   The way of peace, joy and genuine revival

RHP Essential Classics

We Would See Jesus
Seeing in Jesus everything we need
When I Saw Him
Renewing your vision of Jesus
My Calvary Road
Roy Hession tells his own story

F. & M. HOWARD TAYLOR
The Biography of James Hudson Taylor
The life of a man of God

JAMES HUDSON TAYLOR
Union and Communion
Our relationship with Christ from the Song of Songs

F. B. MEYER
The Secret of Guidance
Knowing God's will in every step of life

ANDREW MURRAY
Absolute Surrender
A call to radical, Spirit-filled Christianity
The Full Blessing of Pentecost
Power from on High
Humility
The way to victory in the Christian life
Let Us Draw Near
Entering and experiencing the presence of God
The True Vine
Fruitfulness and stability in Jesus
Waiting on God
Allowing the power of God into our lives and ministries

RHP Essential Classics

OSWALD J. SMITH
  The Enduement of Power
  Being filled with the Holy Spirit
  The Man God Uses
  How anyone can be used powerfully by God
  The Revival We Need
  A heart-stirring cry for revival

R. A. TORREY
  How to Pray
  Praying with power and authority
  How to Study the Bible
  Profit and pleasure from the Word of God

AN UNKNOWN CHRISTIAN
  The Kneeling Christian
  One of the great classics on prayer

DAVID WILKERSON
  Hallowed Be Thy Names
  Knowing God through His names
  Hungry For More of Jesus
  The way of intimacy with Christ

Available from all good Christian retailers

RHP Essential Classics

The School of Christ
by T. Austin-Sparks

Introduction by DAVID WILKERSON

"Are you moving on in the growing fullness of the revelation of the Lord Jesus? Have you an open heaven? Is God in Christ revealing Himself to you in ever greater wonder and fullness?

The ministry contained in this little book has been wrought on the anvil of deep and drastic dealings of God with the vessel. It is not only doctrinal: it is experiential. Only those who really mean business with God will take the pains demanded to read it.

Of all the books that have issued from this ministry, I regard this one as that which goes most deeply to the roots and foundations of our life in Christ with God.

May He make the reading of it result in a fuller understanding of the meaning of Christ."

—T. AUSTIN-SPARKS

"This is a book you will want to read many times. It was during my third reading that its truth fully dawned on me. It has affected my preaching, my outlook on life, and intensified my hunger for the glorious liberty of the Cross. We believe this book is destined by God to bless and edify numerous spiritually hungry ministers and laymen."

—DAVID WILKERSON

RHP Essential Classics

When I Saw Him
by Roy Hession

"In the opening chapters of the Book of Revelation the Apostle John tells us how on the Isle of Patmos he was given an awesome vision of the Lord Jesus, risen from the dead. Then John says, 'When I saw Him, I fell at His feet as dead.' He tells us not only the vision itself, but the profound effect it had on him. It utterly prostrated him before the Lord until He came and laid His right hand on him and said 'Fear not.'"

—ROY HESSION

If we are ever to come to a place of revival, we need to see the Lord as He really is: reigning resplendent in glory and holiness. It is only then that we will see ourselves as we really are and so see our need for Him. In this profound book, Roy Hession looks at three men and a group of men, and the effect that a new vision of the Lord had upon them.

"I had the joy of a close friendship with Roy Hession and saw him putting into practice the message of his books. He is now with the Lord but his message is as relevant as ever."

—GEORGE VERWER
Founder, Operation Mobilisation

Roy Hession's first book, The Calvary Road, has been an international best-seller, with over a million copies sold.